NO B.R. MOVEMENT
BEYOND THIS POINT
WITHOUT PERMISSION
OF CAPTAIN.

Railways
& Recollections

Contents

Series Introduction

Welcome to a brand new and innovative series!

Railway publishing has been around almost as long as the railways themselves and there have been countless books with a historical theme, telling the story of a particular line, say, and occasionally linking the subject to its social context, but never before has there been, in such an accessible way, a juxtapositioning of photographic illustration of a railway subject with the events, happenings and highlights of a wider sphere and calendar. This series will, initially, take a particular year and place the views displayed alongside a carefully selected pot-pourri of what happened in that twelve-month period. The vast majority of the images in the first few books are from the Ray Ruffell collection, held by the publisher, but material from other sources will be interspersed where felt necessary

to maintain appropriate variety. Ray was a railwayman and photographer of equal merit and the main criterion for inclusion in these books is for the images to be both interesting and aesthetically pleasing within a chosen theme.

The books are aimed at a more general market than mere railway aficionados or enthusiasts and the authors hope and trust that they will be sure in their aim and that you, the reader, will find much to enjoy, appreciate, enthuse about and even smile about! And it is hoped that some of your own memories are stirred along the way and that you may wish to share these with friends!

First published in 2006
ISBN 1 85794 277 9   ISBN 978 1 85794 277 4
Silver Link Publishing Ltd
The Trundle
Ringstead Road
Great Addington
Kettering
Northants NN14 4BW

Tel/Fax: 01536 330588
email: sales@nostalgiacollection.com
Website: www.nostalgiacollection.com
British Library Cataloguing in Publication Data
A catalogue record for this book is available from the British Library.
Printed and bound in Great Britain

Above **MOORSWATER** Looking for all the world like some abandoned cathedral are, in truth the remains of Brunel's original, timber-topped Moorswater Viaduct, spanning the valley. Part of one pillar of the replacement eight-arched structure that now carries the Great Western main line from Plymouth to Penzance can be seen on the right.

Frontispiece **THATCHER'S BRANCH?** At this time the railways had an uncertain future epitomised by this view. Were the lines heading for oblivion or would we return to an era of growth and expansion akin to previous halcyon days?

The sign appears to be somewhat optimistic about any movement beyond this point - with or without permission from the captain!

Introduction
Railways & Recollections
1981

The year began with a strange mix of events. Ronald Reagan became President of the USA and Iran responded by releasing 52 previously held US hostages. This 'high' could have been short-lived, however, as Reagan was shot on March 30 by John Hinckley Jr – thankfully, not fatally! America also led the world in space, launching the first and innovative Space Shuttle, less than a month after three were killed and five injured during a Shuttle test. Also in America, the first recognised cases of AIDS are diagnosed. Elsewhere, Greece entered the EEC; Sheffield police arrested the Yorkshire Ripper; a 6.7 magnitude earthquake hit Athens; there were riots in Brixton; Francois Mitterand became France's new Prime Minister; and on July 29, Prince Charles married Lady Diana Spencer.

Bob Dylan turned 40 this year, but newcomers (as babies) included Rapper Mike Jones, tennis stars Anna Kournikova and Serena Williams; and Britney Spears. Elsewhere in entertainment, the FA Cup proved to be memorable as the 100th such occasion and only the second to end in a draw, on the day, since 1912. The replay was finally a victory for Tottenham Hotspur, 3-2 against Manchester City. In music, the year opened with an emotional swell following the assassination of John Lennon the year before, putting the man and his timeless anthem Imagine at the top of the charts for four weeks in January. Other high flyers, later in 1981, were Smokey Robinson Being With You, Michael Jackson One Day In Your Life and Queen & David Bowie Under Pressure. Queen also had the distinction of being the first rock band to play stadiums in South America, breaking the world attendance record with their opening concert in Sao Paulo – 131000!

On our railways, another 53 lines, spurs and/or services were axed. As in some previous years, the predominant casualty was either freight services or links to industrial sites, although passenger services between Kentish Town and Upper Holloway, Newcastle Central and South Shields, Stourport to Hartlebury and New Holland to Barton on Humber and Cleethorpes also suffered. Faslane in Scotland lost its rail link; as did New Hucknall Colliery; Cholsey & Moulsford to Wallingford; and Wednesbury Central to Swan Village. This was also the year that finally saw the end of the famed ECML 'Deltics' in full front line service, with just three of the original 22 locomotives surviving into 1982 (and then only by a matter of days, for celebratory tours, etc.).

Your authors hope you enjoy the mix and will, like Oliver, come back for more!

John Stretton
Oxfordshire

Peter Townsend
Northamptonshire

April 2006

Background **COOMBE JUNCTION**
Coombe Junction station is immediately to the south of Moorswater Viaduct and is the point where trains between Liskeard and Looe have to reverse to continue their journeys. The diminutive single platform station opened in 1901, when the loop to Liskeard was opened and replaced an earlier station nearby at Moorswater. Incredibly, though extremely isolated, it is still open at the time of writing!

1981
Liskeard to Looe

Left **LISKEARD** Shirt sleeves and summer skirts are the order of the day on the 'up' (London-bound) platform at Liskeard as the weak sunshine greets the unidentified Class 50 arriving from Plymouth. As may be surmised from the signage on both platforms, this is the exchange station for Looe branch trains.

When the Liskeard & Looe Railway opened the line to this location, it built the terminus station at right angles to this main line. For trains wishing to visit the branch, access is via the single curve swinging to the left, just above the rear of the Class 50. Passengers need to walk to the end of the 'up' platform and round the far end of the left-hand tree line. Note how clean and tidy everywhere looks at this time.

1981 Happenings (1)

JANUARY

- Peter Sutcliffe 'The Yorkshire Ripper' arrested in Sheffield.
- Caning banned in all Inner London Education Authority Secondary schools
- 52 US hostages held for 14 months in US Embassy in Tehran, Iran released.

LISKEARD Now literally on ground level, off the end of the 'down' platform and looking back towards the B3254 Liskeard-St Keyne roadbridge, we join the tot in its grandma's arms on the opposite platform in watching HST set 253040 enter with a Paddington-bound train. On introduction in the mid-1970s, the HST power cars were allocated sequential set numbers – 253xxx for Western Region and 252xxx for Eastern Region – but it was fairly soon discovered that operational juggling of the cars meant that the set numbers became increasingly meaningless and they were effectively abandoned.

LISKEARD As mentioned on p.5, the Liskeard & Looe Railway station was at right angles to the main line, which is at the far end of the branch platform shown here. Local, Plymouth Class 118 DMU set P470 waits in the alternative Liskeard station, having safely delivered its passenger contingent, who are now making their way through to the main line platforms. The photographer's family patiently wait for him!

1981
No 1 Records

January
There's no one quite like Grandma — St Winifred's School Choir
Imagine — John Lennon

February
Woman — John Lennon
Shaddap you face — Joe Doice Music Theatre

March
Jealous Guy — Roxy Music
This old house — Shakin Stevens

April
Making your mind up — Bucks Fizz

May
Stand and deliver — Adam and the ants

June
Being with you — Smokey Robinson
One day in your life — Michael Jackson

July
Ghost town — Specials

August
Green door — Shakin Stevens
Japanese boy — Aneka

September
Tainted love — Soft Cell
Prince charming — Adam & The Ants

October
It's my party — Dave Stewart & Barbara Gaskin

November
Every little thing she does is magic — Police
Under pressure — Queen & David Bowie

December
Begin the beguine — Julio Iglesias
Don't you want me — Human League

Main pic **COOMBE JUNCTION** A return to the basement level tracks in the Moorswater valley gives some idea of the height of the Viaduct. Those surviving Brunel pillars are again seen, evidencing the gap filled by the wooden top tiers to bring it up to the level of the later viaduct beyond. The angle of view, the wide arches and the shallow topping makes for a very spindly appearance to the viaduct and yet it has carried increasingly heavy trains for well over a century.

Inset left A portrait of the very short platform at Coombe Junction, with a narrow road bridge and viaduct beyond and the facilities for waiting passengers being somewhat sparse!

Inset – right The view from slightly further back from the viaduct, looking with our back towards Coombe Junction station, we capture an HST crossing the viaduct. A further pillar from the erstwhile wooden trestle viaduct is revealed.

COOMBE JUNCTION:.

No 2 Ground Frame was installed after the closure of the signalbox in 1981 to control catch points on the single line freight branch to Moorswater. In the days of steam there was a run-round loop at the station but after the arrival of DMUs this was not required. The ground frame can be seen in the foreground, in this view looking towards Moorswater Viaduct. Note typical Cornish granite bridge to the right.

Right **COOMBE JUNCTION:** No.1 Ground Frame has controlled matters at the southern end of the station area since 1981. Looking towards the station, note the occupation crossing protected by metal gates beyond the cabin. The junction of the line to Looe with the steeply graded section from Liskeard is immediately behind the photographer. *Left*

COOMBE JUNCTION Our final look at Coombe Junction shows another Plymouth DMU three-car set, P432, pausing for trade on the way back to Liskeard. Telltale signs of the old loop line are evident in the presence of old, discarded sleepers and the indentations on the ground of previous sleepers. The climb to Liskeard will start just around the far bend.

Left **LOOE Class118** DMU set P470, seen previously on p.7 at Liskeard, has now wound its way down the slopes and round the bends and is on the final approach to Looe station on 20 August. To the right, boats lie at anchor at low tide, on the tidal estuary of the East Looe River. Just beyond, a 19th century low-arched bridge crosses the estuary and provides a course for the A387 road. While current trade is predominantly tourism, the original raison d-être of the railway was to serve both the fishing port and as an outlet for local mines and quarries.

1981
Happenings (2)

JANUARY

- British Aerospace formed as a PLC
- Greece joins the EEC
- Ronald Reagan elected 40th US President

FEBRUARY

- Athens and surrounding area rocked by Earthquake measuring 6.9 magnitude
- Buckingham Palace announce the engagement of Prince Charles and Lady Diana Spencer
- Plan to close 23 pits abandoned by UK Government

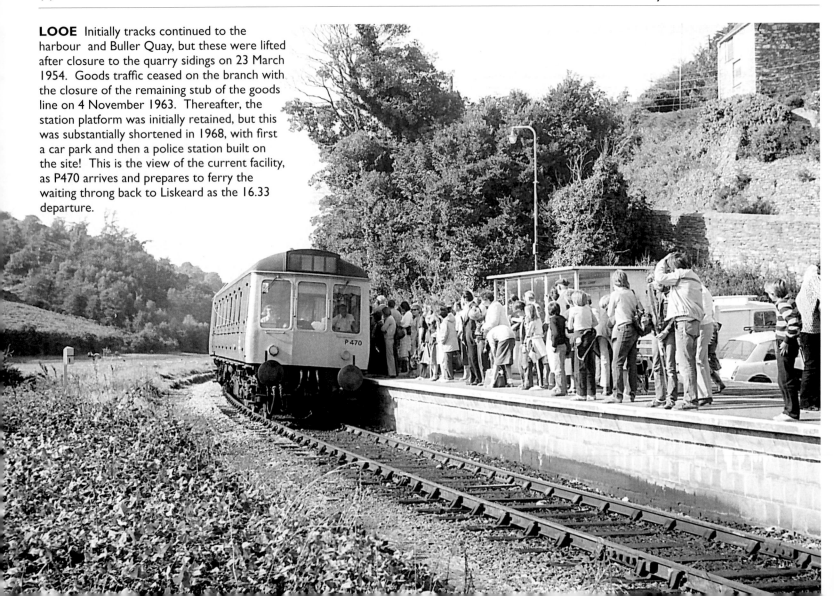

LOOE Initially tracks continued to the harbour and Buller Quay, but these were lifted after closure to the quarry sidings on 23 March 1954. Goods traffic ceased on the branch with the closure of the remaining stub of the goods line on 4 November 1963. Thereafter, the station platform was initially retained, but this was substantially shortened in 1968, with first a car park and then a police station built on the site! This is the view of the current facility, as P470 arrives and prepares to ferry the waiting throng back to Liskeard as the 16.33 departure.

Below ARDROSSAN SOUTH BEACH
Ardrossan might not seem a candidate
for automatic consideration as a holiday
destination, but there are long stretches of
sand along this part of the Ayrshire coast, just
south of the Firth of Clyde, in Scotland. In
addition, just off the North Bay coast is the
Nature Reserve of Horse Isle island. South
Beach station, on the long G&SWR branch
from Kilwinning to Largs, is convenient for
the flattened horseshoe that is South Bay,

with a castle and museum close by. A Largs-
Kilwinning DMU service enters the station
from the north on 15 March, passing under the
B728, one of the town to beach roads. The
branch to Winton Pier swings left immediately
after the roadbridge.

SIGNALLING NOTES *Many railway modellers
will say that a 'train set' becomes a model railway
when signals, are added - preferably working ones!
There is much of interest for the modeller here. On
the left is an unusual gantry having two standard
'home starters' but in the centre is a shunting*

1981
Signals, semaphores and signalboxes

*'dolly' arm controlling restricted movement within
the section. On the right is a single post with three
'dolly' signals these control movement to the three
sidings, beyond the bridge. The top arm controls
the left hand siding the middle arm the middle
siding and the lower arm the right hand siding.
The signal box height ensures a good view over the
bridge. Great telegraph poles too!*

Lower Right We have plenty of Ray Ruffell's
work in these volumes, but here is the man
himself, captured enjoying a footplate ride during
his trip to Scotland.

Below **EARLSWOOD** Inevitably, with the disparate array of original railway companies, designs of signalboxes varied greatly. As well as being primarily functional, some were more aesthetically attractive than others. Earlswood, immediately south of Redhill on the ex-LB&SCR line to Brighton is enhanced by the brick base, bright paint and sliding windows.

Right **BARONY JUNCTION** In complete contrast, the much smaller box at Barony Junction has a far more austere feel, perched on its embankment.

MODELLING NOTES Earlswood box is worthy of close study - note the 'verandah', the outward opening door, handrail and steps construction. The finial is also worthy of note. There are considerable detailing points to note with Baroney Jcn - point rodding with wooden walkway over, short protective fence at the foot of the steps,

the tumbledown sheds, the position of the name plate - not on the front, not beneath the roof eaves but on the side above an interesting door to the 'interlocking room'. The chimney, ornate bracketed shelf, cable junction box and telegraph pole complete the potential for a cameo piece of modelling on any layout!

TONDU Busy junctions required more signals and, hence, larger signalboxes. Tondu Middle junction signalbox in Mid Glamorgan is a case in point, being the conflux of branches from all four main points of the compass. Equipped in 1884 with 65 levers, the frame was renewed as late as 1963. In this view, the driver of Class 37 No. 37245 concentrates on the view behind as he gingerly reverses his long rake of empty coal wagons up the northern route, which once boasted several collieries.

Opposite page If any manual signalbox can be said to be 'typical', this could be it. As well as the 37 levers (numbers varied greatly, as might be expected), there are the various token machines, bells, buttons and warning devices that would be in everyday use. Note the rudimentary chair and table, with train log ledger in place, the metal frame holding the levers (bottom left) and just a glimpse (top centre) of the map board showing the route under the control of this box.

Below **MANCHESTER SHIP CANAL** (MSC) As well as the signals and signalboxes already seen in this section, this portrait captures a rare item of interest but of no less fascination. Swingbridges were not unknown on our railway system, but their number was small in comparison with other, more normal operations. It would appear that this one is partially open, as the tracks that contain MSC's Hudswell 0-6-0 shunter No. D6 end abruptly this side of the bridge!

1981 Happenings (3)

MARCH

- First London Marathon run from Greenwich Park to Buckingham Palace (26 miles)
- President Reagan shot and injured outside Washington D.C. hotel
- Ronnie Biggs the Great Train Robber is kidnapped. Later rescued by Barbados Police and allowed back to Brazil
- SDP (Social Democratic Party) formed

APRIL

- Bobby Sands elected as MP for Fermanagh & South Tyrone. His hunger strike continues
- Brixton Riots - protesters demand end to government's SUS law (Stop and Search)
- Space shuttle Columbia launched - first manned flight by US in almost 6 years

MAY

- Bobby Sands MP dies in prison as a result of his hunger strike
- Pope John Paul II shot in St Peter's Square
- Francois Mitterand elected President of France
- The Yorkshire Ripper jailed for life on 13 counts of murder
- Italian Government resigns

Although signalboxes certainly could look very attractive when working, when closed and abandoned they could easily take on a derelict air. This one once found employment guarding operations through the station in the fork of the two routes. The station has obviously been closed for some time, as the platforms have lost most of their edging stones and any station buildings seem to have disappeared.

On the ground there has obviously been some track relaying – and even realignment? – and the wooden crossing used by the signaller to give and receive single line tokens has been curtailed.

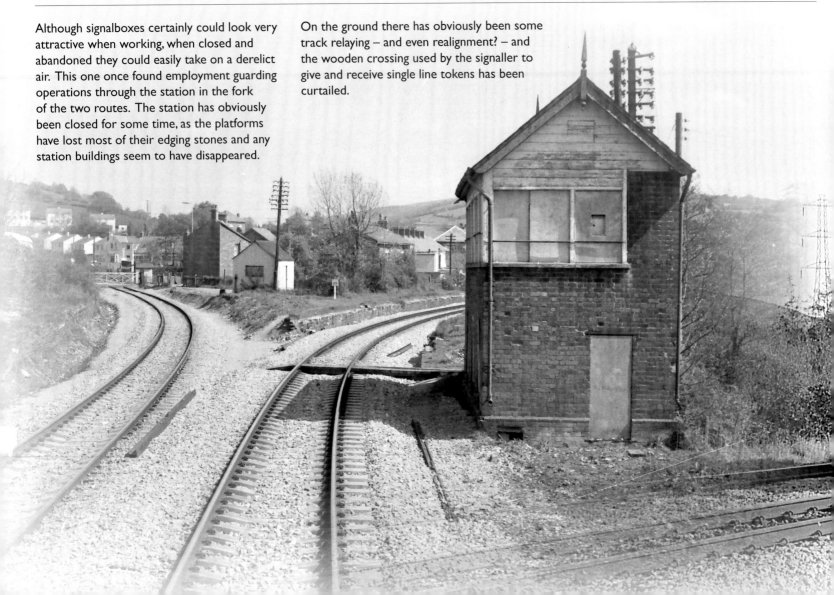

One traffic flow that has survived through to the 21ˢᵗ century is oil. The tanks are large and the weight of trains consequently heavy, requiring main power to haul them. An unidentified Class 47 loco heads westwards along the ex-GWR main line, its way ahead cleared by the typical GWR lower quadrant semaphore signal, which the train has just passed. The other semaphores control the loop line in the foreground, with one route being to sidings on the right.

1981
Rail Rover to
Ipswich

IPSWICH On 20 February, Ray took a trip to Ipswich. Whilst there he was pleased to witness and photograph one of BR's once numerous '03' shunters. With Driver Stan De'ath peering from his cab, the loco crosses a bridge down by the docks. Originally D2179

and new on 20 January 1962, to Hither Green depot on the SR, the TOPS number was received in December 1973, at which time it was still working south of the Thames. A move northeast saw it in Essex and an initial withdrawal at Norwich on 5 July 1987. It was then transferred to Departmental stock, as No. 97807, until February 1989, when it was returned to capital stock. An end to BR work came on 29 October 1993 at Ryde on the Isle of Wight. Amazingly a further lease of life lay ahead for this much travelled little loco. The Train Operating Company WAGN needed a

shunter at their Hornsey depot and reverting to its original number, 03179 was back on track! The loco that refuses to die was named *Clive* at Kings Cross on 25 September 1998, after Clive Allison the retiring maintenance supervisor at Hornsey. The loco is famously the only Class 03 out of 230 built to remain in main line service at the time of writing, (May 2006), although several are preserved. Not bad when withdrawals of class members Started in 1968! No 03179 passed from WAGN to First Capital Direct Ltd., On their taking over the franchise, in April 2006.

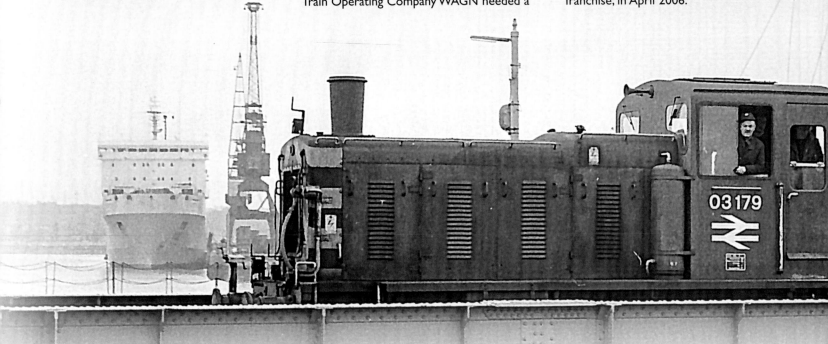

Left **IPSWICH** Somewhat squashed into the locos cab for their portrait are, left to right, Messrs. De'ath, Girling, Scharmann, Mayes and Smith! All seem to be enjoying the experience!

1981
Happenings (4)

JUNE

- Israeli Air Force bombs and destroys Iraqi nuclear generation plant
- HM The Queen shot at by teenager at Trooping the Colour ceremony gun found to contain blanks
- John Lennon's assasin pleads guilty
- Train crash in India results in over 700 dead as train plunges into the River Kosi

JULY

- Riots in Toxteth area of Liverpool results in police use of CS gas for first time to control civil unrest in England
- PLO headquarters in Beirut destroyed by Israeli bombing
- Prince Charles and Lady Diana Spencer marry on 29th July

AUGUST

- MTV launched - *Video killed the Radio Star* by *The Buggles* is first music video shown.
- US Air traffic controllers dispute results in President Reagan sacking over 11,000 employees
- Angola invaded by South Afican troops

IPSWICH DOCKS To complete our trip to the dock area at Ipswich, we find '03' No. 03179 in operation. One of Ray's companions enjoys a cab ride, as a rake of condemned bolster wagons – note the letters 'COND' painted on the wagons sides – is shunted, apparently to separate the first two wagons from the rest. Note the empty shedcode holder on the rear-cab end sheet, between the two windows and just below the top light. In earlier days this would have been complete with the relevant code for the shunter's base depot.

1981 Happenings (5)

SEPTEMBER

- US Steam locomotive *John Bull* claims record for the oldest (150 years) locomotive able to steam and propel iself
- France abolishes capital punishment

OCTOBER

- Hunger strikes at Maze Prison end
- Egyptian President Anwar Sadat assasinated
- CND march in London attracts over 250,000 protesting over siting of nuclear missiles in Britain
- Andreus Papandreou elected as Greek Prime Minister
- Hosni Mubarak elected President of Egypt

More views on Ray's 20 February visit to the area.

Left **IPSWICH** Another Class 03 at Ipswich and numerically the one after that seen on p.22. On Station Pilot duty, in case of emergencies, No. 03180 stands close by the DMU seen opposite.

Below left **IPSWICH DOCKS** Seen from the cab of 03179 – see p.22 – and looking extremely sad, forlorn and abandoned, this diminutive shunter has been dumped at the end of an out-of-the-way siding in Ipswich Docks. The sad condition of the neighbouring buildings and yard do nothing to lift the sprits!

Below right **GRIFFIN WHARF** Recognising the heavier loads handled at Griffin Wharf freightliner terminal, close to Halifax Junction on the main line and Ipswich Tunnel, 08661 – a more powerful Class 08 locomotive than the '03s' – shunts a rake of open wagons containing a variety of items. Ray's companions give the loads slightly closer examination.

IPSWICH At the time of writing, Ipswich is an important station on the ex-GER main line from Norwich to Liverpool Street, with three busy branches, to Felixstowe, Bury St Edmunds and Lowestoft. It is also a stabling point for locomotives operated by the Freightliner rail company. Seen from the yard, with the delightfully scalloped canopy design, yet another variant of DMU is seen having just arrived in Platform 4 on 20 February.

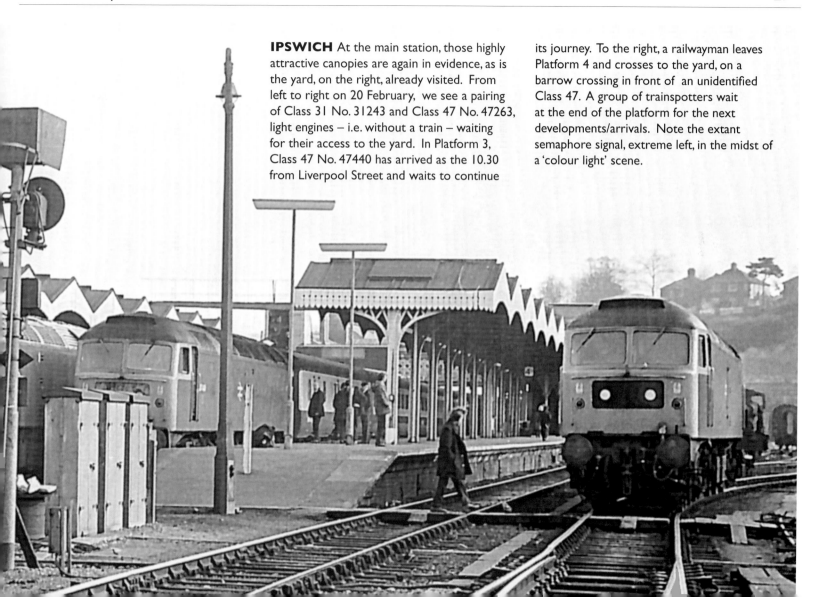

IPSWICH At the main station, those highly attractive canopies are again in evidence, as is the yard, on the right, already visited. From left to right on 20 February, we see a pairing of Class 31 No. 31243 and Class 47 No. 47263, light engines – i.e. without a train – waiting for their access to the yard. In Platform 3, Class 47 No. 47440 has arrived as the 10.30 from Liverpool Street and waits to continue its journey. To the right, a railwayman leaves Platform 4 and crosses to the yard, on a barrow crossing in front of an unidentified Class 47. A group of trainspotters wait at the end of the platform for the next developments/arrivals. Note the extant semaphore signal, extreme left, in the midst of a 'colour light' scene.

Right top **DIDCOT** As one travelled the country by rail, whether as enthusiast or ordinary passenger, it was amazing how many 'extraordinary' items of rolling stock were around. Many were from earlier times. Such as this ex-Gresley LNER coach, here as Departmental QPV No. DE 320893, seen at Didcot on 6 February. Originally numbered E16065E, it was in use here as a Civil Engineer Staff and Dormitory coach to accompany engineering works. Either side are Ballast Cleaner No. DR 76319 and box van.

Right bottm **DIDCOT** The Ballast Cleaner glimpsed above is here in its entirety at Didcot on 6 February, still in company with its ex-LNER coach. DR 76319, new in 1979, is one of 23 Plasser & Theurer RM 74 machines constructed between 1978 and 1983 and basically mechanised the job of cleaning all ballast under the tracks that had been all but impossible for older, manual operations. Self-contained, it transformed the 'bed' of the railway, leading to safer and faster trains.

If visiting DIDCOT we highly recommend a visit to:

The Didcot Railway Centre

Home of the Great Western Society and its unique collection of Great Western Railway steam engines, coaches, wagons, buildings and small relics and a recreation of Brunel's broad gauge railway.

1981
Steam age relics keep hi-tech company!

Right **SWINDON** Same date but different location. Seen at Swindon, 20 ton ex-brakevan No. DW 17466 stands in a siding, now used as a Mess & Tool Van for the Soil Mechs Sect. BRB. Note the instruction 'No Hump Shunt', referring back to the heyday of marshalling yards when gravity from a hump was used to separate wagons.

Below **SWINDON** Yet another example of past and present. Still in service on BR on 6 February, this distinctly ancient-looking 20T ex-GWR Swindon-built crane was constructed in 1911! Travelling with it is a 'match' wagon No. ADB 735877.

When in **Swindon** *be sure to try and visit:*

STEAM

Museum of the Great Western Railway

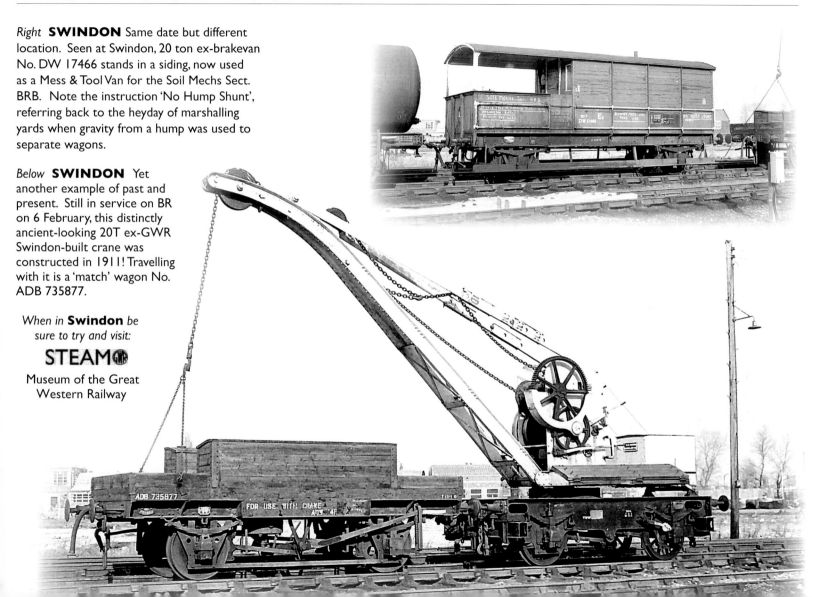

1981
Happenings (6)

NOVEMBER

- Berlin Wall demolition begins signalling the end of the Cold War
- USA and Soviet Union begin talks in Geneva on nuclear weapons reduction
- Early reports of what is now known to be AIDS start appearing in UK press and media

DECEMBER

- Penlee Lifeboat *The Solomon Brown* lost with all hands off the Cornish coast in a heroic rescue attempt to save the crew of *The Union Star* also lost with all hands.

LARGS 'Cancer Kills Old <u>and</u> Young Everywhere…' Although laudable as a notice to encourage donations for research, not exactly the kind of sign that the travelling public might want to greet them at the station, especially when so close to posters for a Health Race and wedding attire! Let us hope that the two cyclists on Largs forecourt on 15 March are fit and healthy and in no danger of the dreaded disease! A wonderful panoramic scene of the terminus station at a busy time.

1981
Multiples on manoeuvres

Opposite **LARGS** Walking onto the platforms, the DMUs are temporarily stationary at Largs on 15 March. Scottish sets 129 and 136 are poised to take their next complements of passengers south, with set No.144 in the siding as backup. A relatively simple station, without the grandeur already seen at other places in this series of books, there is still ample cover provided for any waiting travellers.

Left **WINDSOR** Many railway stations have been used as backdrops for films, both TV and big screen, with the vast majority featuring steam. Not so here! Which one is being created here is unknown, but the tell-tale temporary rails laid on the platform at Windsor & Eton Riverside station show that the activity is underway, with actors and film crew congregating by the open doors of Class 415/1 4EPB No. 5112. Dating from March 1954, the unit is not in public service here but was returned to BR after filming, with three of the four coaches reformed into unit 5492 in August 1986.

Opposite and below **ARDROSSAN HARBOUR** The weather may have been terrible but, thankfully, Ray did not put away either his camera or his photographic eye! Indeed, the reflections created by the torrential rain have actually added to the overall effect.

Inside the aesthetically-challenged exterior of Ardrossan Harbour station, Scottish DMU set 154 endures the cold, wet evening before forming the 18.05 'Boat Train' (!) to Glasgow on 17 March.

Left **GATWICK AIRPORT** The bright summer morning light is used to good advantage here, as Class 421 4CIG No. 7359 restarts its journey from Victoria to Ore via Eastbourne (code 52). Originally built in the 1960s as one of the batch of 30 four-car units to operate on the Waterloo–Portsmouth services 7359 was new in October 1970 and it, too, was later renumbered, to 1259 in June 1987 after the removal of asbestos. In the background, a DMU stands in the adjacent platform, having arrived from Reading.

Below **WATERLOO** The Class 508s were offsprings of the successful PEP prototypes – see p.13 of the 1973 volume in this series – and 43 sets were built at BR's Works in York between 1979 and 1981. Initially delivered to the SR as four-car, the early units were reduced to three cars by the end of 1981 and the whole class had been transferred to Merseyside by 1985, where they replaced ageing Class 502 units; the displaced trailers from the four-car sets were used for the Class 455/7 EMUs where they still operate today.

Sets 508025, 508007 and 508013 stand in the Waterloo's cavernous trainshed between duties. The latter two were later returned south and from 1998, renumbered in the 508/2 series, worked for South Central, later Southern trains on the erstwhile SR territory.

1981
Arrivals & Departures

Births

Owen Hargreaves	footballer	20 January
Justin Timberlake	musician	31 January
Lleyton Hewitt	Australian tennis player	24 February
Craig David	singer	5 May
Anna Kournikova	Russian tennis player	7 June
Roger Federer	Swiss tennis player	8 August
Serena Williams	US tennis player	26 September
Milan Baros	footballer	28 October

Deaths

A. J. Cronin	novelist	(b. 1896)	6 January
Bill Haley	musician	(b. 1925)	9 February
Joe Louis	boxer	(b. 1914)	12 April
Bobby Sands	Irish Republican	(b. 1954)	5 May
Bob Marley	singer/musician	(b. 1945)	11 May
Bill Shankly	football manager	(b. 1913)	8 September
Anwar Sadat	President of Egypt	(b. 1918)	6 October
Moshe Dayan	Iraeli general	(b. 1915)	16 October
William Holden	actor	(b. 1918)	16 November
Natalie Wood	actress	(b. 1938)	29 November

Left **NORTH CAMP** The descriptive term for Diesel Electric Multiple Unit (DEMU) – as opposed to DMU and EMU – was explained more fully in the 1973 volume. Compared to the other two types mentioned, the DEMUs were much rarer beasts, usually only operating on non-electrified lines within BR(SR). The bright sunshine again enlivens the view as Class 205 unit No 1306 enters North Camp on the Reading - Redhill line. The casual clothes of the gathered throng indicate a warm summer's day.

1981 was, of course, the year of the wedding of Prince Charles and Lady Diana Spencer. That fact is celebrated in the cab of the Class 119 DMU, with a facsimile of one of the celebratory Royal Mail stamps and a rosette! Set L583 pauses while Ray takes the photograph, with the guard patiently waiting, no doubt aware that there is no dramatic hurry on this North Downs service between Redhill and Reading.

It has been said before, that it is harder to produce an attractive and/or satisfying photograph of our modern railway than it was in steam days, as the added ingredient of the steam and the inherent aesthetics of the steam locomotive are absent. One technique, mastered by renowned photographers such as Brian Morrison, is to place the train in its context. Effectively this means finding an attractive view without the train and then wait for it to arrive, often standing a little further back from the line than would possibly be the norm. This is exactly what has happened here, with the juxtaposition of the houses – both above and below – with the railway and the perfectly placed Class 119 DMU unit on the low viaduct creating a pleasing result.

BARONY COLLIERY In common with so many other parts of the UK, Scotland's coal industry was emaciated with so many closures during the dark days for coal in the 1980s. Barony Colliery in Ayrshire, in southeast Scotland, closed in 1989. In slightly happier times, on 9 March, the driver and secondman of Class 27 No. 27111 pose for their portrait, before they take their well-loaded train away from the colliery. To the left is the NCB Works' Rolls-Royce Sentinel diesel.

Right **BARONY COLLIERY** Moments later and the '27' exerts maximum effort to begin the slog up the steep branch to Barony Junction, viewed from the cab of the Sentinel diesel. The full trainload will then be taken to Ayr Harbour, where it will be transhipped for delivery to Ireland.

1981
Coal & Power by the Wagon load!

Above **BARONY COLLIERY** On 9 March the NCB Sentinel diesel shunts yet more coal at Barony Colliery, with part of the colliery complex to the right. What appears to be a chimney is actually a small coal chute behind the loco!

Right **OGMORE VALLEY** The relatively short branch from Blackmill to Nantymoel in South Wales was virtually littered with collieries in its early days. Again, most had been swept away by the late-1980s but a few, with their attendant facilities, lingered to the end. On 23 April, Class 37 No. 37245 slowly edges forward through the Ogmore Valley Washery.

ASHINGTON COLLIERY More evidence for coal being of massive importance to the railway's balance sheet. Prior to the battle between Mrs Thatcher and Arthur Scargill, and the pit closures that followed the miners' strike of the mid-1980s, collieries and pits – from deep mines to opencast – were liberally scattered around the country. The National Coal Board (NCB) was the operator of a massive organisation, with a fleet of its own locomotives handling traffic within the pit/colliery confines. The BR Type 1 D95xx fleet was very short-lived as, by the time that the locos were being introduced, their planned work was being phased out! 55 were built at Swindon between July 1964 and October 1965 and the first two were withdrawn in December 1967! Hardly a good BR investment! Later to be designated as Class 14 and affectionately known as 'Teddy Bears', many went to the NCB after BR and three are seen here at NCB's Ashington Colliery. Note the winding gear in the background.

LYNEMOUTH An interesting and intriguing picture to end on! 'PAO' alumina hoppers were built in 1971 for the short-distance flow of imported alumina from North Blyth to Lynemouth, in the northeast. They were unfitted and were probably the last unfitted wagons to be built for main-line use. They remained in use until replaced by 'PCA' tank wagons in the late 1980s. Whilst the precise location is unclear, the unidentified Class 37 could well be departing from the Alcan plant at Lynemouth. Whatever the circumstances, the low angle makes for a pleasing image.

Inset **BARONY POWER STATION** One final look at Barony, in southeast Scotland, sees the '27' No. 27111 briefly at the buffer stops, with, presumably, the driver sharing some joke with Ray!

1981
FILMS - A SELECTION

Title	*Director*
• Raiders of the lost ark	Steven Spielberg
• The Boat (Das Boot)	Wolfgang Petersen
• Gallipoli	Peter Weir
• Chariots of fire	David Puttnam
• Body Heat	Lawrence Kasdan
• Reds	Warren Beatty
• An American werewolf in London	Robert Altman
• On golden pond	Mary Rydell
• The French Lieutenant's woman	Karel Reisz

Index

Acknowledgements

As with projects of any size and/or complexity, there are many people 'behind the scenes' who give of their time, expertise, advice, etc. willingly but often receive little in the way of thanks in return. The same is true with this new series, with the exception that the team putting the launch titles together has been smaller than is the norm.

There have been others 'in the wings', but the core personalities who deserve especial mention – apart from the two authors, whose patience, tolerance and friendship have somehow survived long hours, tight deadlines and frustration with some lack of information from the original photographs (!) – are Brian Morrison, for his constant and ever-ready willingness to offer assistance, advice and research facilities and for proof reading so quickly; and Sharon Rich, for her common sense approach and comments. This is her first excursion into the world of publishing and not only has it been eye-opener for her, but she has added a vital ingredient of not being an existing railway enthusiast! She has also coped remarkably well with those same tight deadlines, on top of managing her family and domestic duties!

Paul Shannon and John Vaughan deserve mention for specialist information on specific pictures.

Peter Rowlands is also thanked for his early enthusiasm, encouragement and for helping to drum up outside support; and Connie Ruffell for permission to use one or two specific photographs. Frances Townsend for sustaining her husband through the process! Without these individuals, the project would not have achieved what it already has.